I Am Lucky

A Poetic Odyssey

Bianca Barich

Tellwell Talent
www.tellwell.ca

ISBN

978-1-77302-872-9 (Paperback)
978-1-77302-873-6 (Ebook)

Table of Contents

Chapter 1: BIRTH OF DESIRE...................1

Chapter 2: EXPRESS YOUR TRUE NATURE........13

Chapter 3: DEATH OF MY FEAR...............25

Chapter 4: CONFLICTED BY CHAOS............31

Chapter 5: DIVINE TIME....................41

Chapter 6: EXPLORE YOUR WONDERLAND......51

Chapter 7: THE WAY.......................61

Chapter 8: HEALING THE ILLUSION OF PAIN.....69

Chapter 9: SWEET LOVE....................81

Chapter 10: ILLUMINATING DREAMS...........91

To Eric and Sophia

I Love You
To the Moon and back
I Love You
In between the twinkling stars
I Love You
All around the Sun
Because you are my little one

PREFACE

The following collection of poems is the genesis of my poetic expression. When wondering about my life's experience I can't help but feel an eclectic mix of emotions. I would like to share with you my insights when experiencing euphoria, bliss, and ecstasy. And I would also like to explore the darker tides of time that can often crash our life's course into chaos.

When we wander onto the edge of illusion, the reality we have known before becomes malleable to our liking. When we can grasp the ultimate truth that we have the free will to follow our dreams and make them happen, that is when we can skyrocket into the life we are dying to live. Know that the only one standing in your way is You!

You are the creator of your life.
Do you choose Love or Fear?

My sensitive nature is both a curse and a blessing. My feelings are deep and my experiences are intense. This can be great when I channel myself properly, but when a negative state of mind takes over those deep feelings can escalate into something nasty. My intuitive side sparks a sensational ride through life. I love when my senses guide me on the right path, especially when there are those little clues or meaningful coincidences that encourage me to trust my feelings, because they are always right.

Let your soul speak through your heart's feelings. When you do what soothes and serves the soul, you are well on your way of bringing serenity into your life.

Who is Lucky?

Lucky was a Dalmatian dog that I took care of in the summer of 2008. That was a year of transformation for me. But it was during that fateful summer when my life took a turn in the right direction. While on my many walks with Lucky the dog I started to discover my newfound love, my love of words. Words strung into sentences which followed the rhythm of my heart. This well of inspiration overflowed with bliss. Rebirth, because at that point in my life I felt stuck. Poetry picked me up and got my engine working again. This fuel was like fluid emotion. I truly felt: "I am Lucky"

I walk this path that I have chosen, and every step of the way leads me closer to becoming one with my purpose. The journey my soul set out to travel before I came into existence is a glorious rollercoaster of ups and downs. A molehill becomes a mountain; a single tear can drown me. As I am swept away by an emotional hurricane I can hear the silence in the eye of the storm. Truth becomes apparent: the landscapes of my mind need to be cleansed of ego's chaos.

Now that I am reborn out of the ashes from the fire of destruction, I give birth to a new way of being.

Chapter 1

BIRTH OF DESIRE

Know your desires
Let them guide
Your meditation
They are the infinite
Source of your creation

Heed the whispers
Of the song in life
That's the tune
You must dance to

The only path to walk in life
Is the road heading
Towards who you want to be
You have it all in your hands
Only you can turn the key

The poet in my heart
Whispers in my ear
Embrace the joy in life
Reject the illusion of fear
Maker of dreams
Messenger of
Soulful desire
You are what gives
My heart fire
Passion burns
To fuel purpose
The goal of
A meaningful life

Somewhere in time is a golden place
You may call it your sacred space
Relax and close your eyes
Dream away and visualize
Teach yourself this joyful way
To brighten up your everyday

For love to grace you on your way
You have to be love every day
Love all that is and that is all
Love is the seed where it has begun
To know the truth is to know we are one

Dawn is here
Blessings of a new day
Happiness is near
Joy is on its way
Brighten up your life
With the rays of the sun
Spice up your life
With a whole bunch of fun

6

Pulsating life force
Enveloping all that is
You fill me with love
Into a state of bliss
Vibrating on the
Highest frequency
I don't want to come down

Let the love flow from deep inside
Realize your heart has nothing to hide
Follow your dreams
Before you fall from grace
Be a beacon of light
For the human race

Glorious love you inspire dreams
You show what life is all about
And not just what it seems
Guide me along the way
For my heart will understand
You are the ruler
Of my wonderland

Joy is a gift that you
Receive with an open heart
The gratitude of the soul
Will bless you with this bliss
When the ego is aligned
With the will of the mind
You will open up doors
Seek and you will find

Ignite my fire
With a spark of desire
Let the love we feel
Take us higher
Wasted regrets are here no more
For they are a liar
There is only one true bliss
Let Love Inspire

Unfulfilled desire
It needs to be taken care of
I have to explore all facets of love
To truly live I have to feed
My passions and my need
And thus fill my life
With joyous deed

*My heart is burning
With passion and desire
My love for you is like
A warm glowing fire
Let our hearts be as one
So that together we will
Shine as brightly as the sun*

Chapter 2

EXPRESS YOUR TRUE NATURE

Life is creating a painting
Choose your colours, paint your life
You hold the brush
You control your own destiny

Footprints of your creation
Pave a way to liberation

Every creation is a piece of art
Even the failures
Inspire you to be better
Do things differently next time

14

The birth of my independence
Was not too long ago
What a liberation
Free from my prison
Free from mental manipulation
Oh so long I had waited for change
But it never found me
I realize now
I have to be
True to myself
To truly be free

Communicate your feelings
You have nothing to hide
Show your true self
Let me know what's inside
Give yourself this freedom
Know what is true
Expressing your true self
Is what serves you

Sitting here
Thoughtfully wondering
What to say
Let your inner vision
Guide you on your way
May you find
What you are looking for
Whatever it may be
Follow your dreams
So that they can set you free
I hope you will live out loud

The words I read
In my book of life
Are gentle, caring
And sweet in deed
They are all I need
They are what I heed

18

My sweet creation
You are the poet of my heart
You have given me a new start
Exploring the mind
The way it is supposed to be
Fighting together to
Set my soul free

The secret of living
Can be found
By giving
The gift of life
Can be found
In love
The key to love
Can be found
In your heart
For the love of life
Let go and find
A new start

My head is congested with thoughts full of questions
Every question has a million answers
Which one shall I choose today?
Black or White, Love or Fear, Day or Night
Today I am in a happy mood
With no space for the negative
I wish every day could feel this good

Always have faith
Never take your eyes off the prize
Know that you will reap what you sow
Don't forget you are the cause of your effect
Be aware you are the source of your regret
Yet know you are the engine of your life
Strive to reach full potentiality
And never forget who you want to be

Seasons come, seasons go
Years pass by
Time makes everything grow
But why do you fly?
Sometimes time takes things away
In that case be brave and strong
Know tomorrow is a better day
And pain won't linger long
For those who can't forgive
Try to forget
Darkness is not the way to life
In the end it is not forgiving
That you will regret

Guiding force
Leads us all
Protecting arms
Catch my fall
Caressing hand
Strokes my face
Healing source
Brings love to this place

Chapter 3

DEATH OF MY FEAR

Only fools are ruled
By the fear inside
Love conquers all
And I have
Nothing to hide

A shift has taken place
My fears are gone
I have found my sacred space

Feelings of love
I hold you dear
My heart
Has no place
For fear

To walk the path of life
The way it is supposed to be
Existing in a state of harmony
That is why on your journey of life
Take only what you want and need to grow
Leave the rest behind
There is no place
For the negative, just leave it
And life will treat you kind

Don't deny your highest good
Because you are ruled by
Your deepest fears
Don't let life pass you by
You don't want to regret
Wasted years
Don't cling to the past
It will give you pain
And bring you tears
Don't worry about the future
It will give you wrinkles and grey hair
Now that's no good
Don't be focused on the negative
It will put you in a bad mood
Now learn these lessons
And learn them well
So you don't have to live
In a man-made hell

Death of my fear
Songs of liberation
Freedom is finally here
Moving to another vibration
Attitudes shift before my eyes
Breaking free from the prison of my mind
Released from telling lies
Reaching for what my soul
Is trying to find

Your energy is drawing me near
Those old days are gone
I've finally lost that fear
I'm willing to let you in
My guard is down
My walls are thin
I can truly say with all my heart
I'm ready for a new start

Leave your fears behind
Let your self be free
Love is the infinite source
You are longing to find
She will allow you to be
Who you want to be

Chapter 4

CONFLICTED BY CHAOS

Puzzled by the picture
Portrayal of my past
Passions profoundly
Procrastinated
Pour Qua?

Treat everybody like gold
Unless they have proven
They are only worth lead

Man, the manipulator
Man, the mystery
Man, the interpretation
Man, repeating history

My mind is the prisoner
Of my heart
Afraid of change
Fearful of a new start
I know I have to
Break free, if I want to
Be happy and truly me

If my brain is my mind
My heart is my soul
And God is the world
Why doesn't the world show
My brain that it doesn't
Have to hurt my heart?
Where does that leave my body?
My body is society
I don't blame God
I blame my body
I blame society
I blame me

Why can love hurt?
What is going wrong?
My chains of fear hold you tight
But I need to hold you dear
So it was me all along
To keep love we have to be
Able to set love free
Now I know what to do
To have you stay with me

Patterns of the past
Repeating mistakes
Life goes so fast
Blind to the
Lessons of life
Failing the test

The trap I have created
In my mind won't allow
Me to search for what
I need to find
I know I have to climb this wall
To allow myself to be part of it all

I want to be
At the peak of my
Infinite potentiality
So that finally
I can break free
From this coldhearted
Individuality

Wishing for a better day
Letting go of all my fears
Hoping for a better way
Coping with wasted years
Avoiding pity tears

Change your perception
Of what is good and bad
Don't cling to things
That are sad
Feed on what makes
You glad

Chapter 5

DIVINE TIME

Enhancing the senses
Exploring the mind
Let my heart reach
For what it wants to find

Looking at the world with new eyes
This true healer makes you realize
Let the feelings flow from your heart
And live your life with love

Opening the heart
The mind free
For a new start
Where my soul
Wants to be

42

The eternal battle of Good and Bad
The angel wants what the devil had
The devil desires wings like the angel
So that he can break free
From the bond that hell puts up onto thee
But only the angel knows
The difference between Good and Bad
That's why he deserves his wings
This makes the devil mad
Because he doesn't know these things

43

Free your spirit
Free your mind
Open your eyes
And you will find
Hearken your heart
It will lead the way
Your heart calls you
Where you have to stay

For God to end this world of fear
Something needs to be done
Realizing God is Love
Uniting us as one
Open your heart
Let the love shine through you
Spread it around and receive it back
Let this be what you do

Flowing from the heart
Balancing with the mind
Letting your soul be part
Of what you are trying to find
Inspiration guiding your way
Fueled with passion and desire
Letting your purpose lift you higher

God of day, God of light
Brighten up this year
Let me win the fight
Let me conquer fear
I know that after the darkest night
The sun will be here

The river of time
Washes away
Your sorrow
Seasons change
And so do you
Learn to let go
Live to be true
Seize the opportunity
Of a new day
Life is a gift
What is your present?
Unwrap the joys of love
For she is the true healer

48

Oh Holy Spirit divine
Today I saw another sign
May my life serve you each day
May your love guide me on my way
I feel that I am one with
The one who is all
I feel that it is time to
Break down my wall

Let my heart be aligned
With what my soul is out to find
I hope my journey is filled
With dreams that come true
Love my life
That is all
I need to do

For my soul mate
You are the savior of my soul
You are my strength and my fire
You are my love and my desire
Without you I would
Dwell through endless pain
Without you I would go insane

Chapter 6

EXPLORE YOUR WONDERLAND

The illusion of separateness
And the individuality of self
Must be balanced
With the vision of the mind

Be inspired
Inspire those you can
This is a good way
To help your fellow man

May your journey be bright
And your baggage be light
Whatever life throws at you
Know you will win the fight

Warm gentle breath of life
I adore your golden ray
Like a healing kiss onto my soul
You guide me on my way
Divine spirit light up my flame
And I will fuel it with love
Blessed by your presence
Watching over me from above
Always here, never far
Bringing light in my life
My guiding star

He who dares to dream
Will summon forth
A future brighter
Then you have ever seen
Whatever you may wish for
Whoever you want to be
Live out your dreams
And you will live happily

Provoke your thoughts
Stimulate that brain
Don't let it die in vain
Cherish those
Beautiful memories and
Remember to make more
Because making beautiful
Memories, makes life
Worth living for

You said, you are all
There is in your mind
Footprints of the past
Show you what you need to find
Learn from the mistakes of before
Don't cling
Just let it be
Or else there will be more

Your vessel will sail the course
You have set out before you embarked
Don't struggle against the elements
They will lead you exactly
Where you need to be
Where you will meet destiny

Memories of the past
Question what could come
Will these feelings last?
Where do these fears
Originate from?
Overcoming takes courage
And may bring a change of heart
Stand tall, be strong
And prepare for a new start

58

Secret doorways in your mind
Don't answer when they call
Frustrating illusions
You will find
Down the rabbit hole
You will fall
Unless you are willing
To leave reality behind

Loosing grip of life's
Grandest illusion
Fooled by the space of time
Gravitating towards
The truth, but
Is your truth mine?

Chapter 7

THE WAY

The blades of green
Wave hello
When you make
The wind blow

Mystical metaphors
Morphing into
Magical moralities

Triumphantly smiling
Over my latest, greatest
Victory...

62

I never paid much attention in class
So I was not properly molded that way
Now, if it's ok
I take my liberty and say:
To hell with society, I make my own play

I am the teacher
Of the lessons in life
I am the healer
Of your heart
I am time
I am an illusion
I know only
One truth
You are the savior
Of your soul
Only you can set
Yourself free

The compass of my heart
Guides me to truth
The stormy weather of the
Ocean of my emotion
Throws me off course
The northern star will
Always show the way
No matter how rough my
Experience might stray

In the ebb and flow of my life
The tides take me on a rough ride
Struggling to keep
Head above water
Fear of the unknown abyss
Staring back at me through
The view of empty horizons

I once read: "write your
Worries in sand and carve
Your blessings in stone"
This is beautiful and true
But sometimes it feels my
Life is like the sand
Carried away into the future
On the winds of the past
I don't feel the solid rock
I am fragile as glass
Made by the sand

I stand tall and mighty
Flexible enough not to
Snap in the storm of emotion
I nurture your body, mind and soul
As we exchange the breath of life
My roots go deep
Making sure to break up
The stagnant parts of your being
Our foundation grows stronger
As we synthesize the light of Love
Unite with me
I am the tree of life
I bear the fruits of your labour

I planted the seed of courage a long time ago
But the coward in me did not have the strength
To let my sun shine
Hunted by grey clouds of disappointment
My anger roars with thunder
And then, thoughts collide
Negative and positive find equilibrium
And the emotions start to pour
Nourishing the seed
At last the tension is gone
The clouds have disappeared
My sun is ready to fuel my courage
The seed has sprouted

Chapter 8

HEALING THE ILLUSION OF PAIN

The fiction of my addiction
The illusion of my pain
Got to stop thinking about it
Or I will go insane

Tears of a stone cold heart
Truth is the illusion of the liar
Truth is the perception of the illusion
The truth of life is in pursuing your destiny

Slightly slipping through
The gates of insanity
Exploring borders of the mind
Playing with su-real-ity

The fear in your mind
Will project fear
Into your world
The truth in your heart
Will illuminate
The illusion of fear
Accepting the illusion will
Bring us back to the garden
The love in your heart
Will project love
Into your world
Love is the only
Truth in life
Don't live in the illusion
Accept the truth

Lost on the familiar streets
Of memory lane
The past has paved a road
To nowhere
Dead end
Around the corner
Is a shortcut
Roadblocks ahead
But the final destination
Is in sight

Wondrous ignorance
Why have you burdened
Me with your bliss?
Constantly fooled by
Your flawed failures
Consciously creating chaos
Intelligence ignoring ignorance
Destroying that ego demon

Always in a hurry
Rushing from A to B
Living life with tunnel vision
Never being what you want to be
Losing sight of goals and dreams
Forgetting the most important
Part of it all

The beauty of your being
Only goes skin deep
Satisfied by the empty thoughts
Of your shallow mind
So much room to grow
But blinded by ignorance
Searching for truth
In the wrong places
Judgment clouded by
An insecure heart
Hiding away behind
Your sharp tongue

Prisoners of the mind
Open your heart by
Breaking free from
The boundaries of ego
So the soul can search
For your destiny

Walking down memory lane
Gazing upon fields of sacrifice
Recalling regrets
But never for the worse
The ego suffers
The heart is free

Trail of broken promises
Leads me to a land of loss
Searching for a graceful galaxy
Filled with brighter stars
Longing for a Universe
Ruled by Love

Healing comes with change
Because obviously
Your old pattern doesn't serve you
Draw from within
For without the inner strength
We are just an outer shell
A shadow of greater potential

Walk tall, chin up, and smile
Blessed by another beautiful day
Forget your fears
It's all in your head
Your observation
Life is what you make of it
Make life happen
Your way

The past me has skillfully
Crafted me into the entity
That I am today
There are some errors of regret
But I am almost past the shame
Factoring the melodrama
That comes with the human mind
I must say I am pretty happy
With the woman I am today

Chapter 9

SWEET LOVE

Get the most out of your pleasure
For this will heal your sorrow
Live out your dreams
For a better tomorrow

Things are not always what they seem
Will you see with the same eyes
After your heart has open up?

Morning Glory bless us
With your loving light
Warm up my day
After this long cold night

Reunite in Paradise
Thought waves filled with feelings of love
An intent so sweet and pure coming straight from
the heart
That sacred space belongs to you
Where the birth of my creation reached for the stars
Out there it can shine so brightly among its brothers
and sisters
Together in perfect harmony
Let us all align our thoughts
Open our heart and tune in to the ultimate frequency
Maybe then humanity will shine as brightly as those
beautiful stars
That light up the dark night
Then we can bring heaven to earth
And reunite in Paradise

Reflections of our Love
Good things that were
Better things to come
The only reflection
I want to see is
You and Me
Happily

84

Warm glowing light in me
I love when you
Make me sparkle
My soul smiles from within
I want to show you the
World through the eyes of God
The way it is meant to be

Brilliant, shining, like the
Reflections in an ocean of love
Solid, like the rock around my finger
Unbreakable, sparkling into eternity
What we have is even more
Than this, it is true
Love at first sight, and the rest
Comes naturally

Tears of joy
They taste sweet
Instead of salty
They fill your heart
With warmth and love
They make you glow
Oh please let me drown
In this sweet ocean of love

Passionate hearts
Be wild and free
Don't get stuck in routine
Let there be that
Ever burning flame
Warming love
Eternally ours
Because our love
Is stronger than death

Soulful wisdom
Intuitively received
Through blissful knowing
Gracefully expressing
Universal truths
And divine knowledge

Today I celebrate the birth
Of my newfound creativity
So grateful for that spark of desire
That sets this poetry engine in motion
Fulfillment brings serenity to my soul
I never want to let go of you, my Venus

Fill my mind with knowing
Fill my soul with being
Fill my heart with Love
Remove all obstructions
From my body and thought

Chapter 10

ILLUMINATING DREAMS

Thanks for guiding me
On this path that I walk
Thanks for listening
When I talk

Thank you, Mother Earth
For your nurturing, solid love
Thank you, Father Sky
For lifting my soul so high

Thank you for your power
Thank you for the darkest hour
Thank you for what you have done
Now I know that you and I are one

92

My soul walks this karmic
Journey through the
Cycles of life and death
Seeking to perfect itself
Gaining wisdom
Through experience
Putting life to the test
Living through joy and pain
On an everlasting quest
Trying to balance
GO...O...D *&* *D...*EVIL

What are your pleasures?
Dream them out in your fantasy world
Let them lighten up your day
Use your creative expressions
And with focused intention
They will come your way

Words are misconceptions
Of feelings and ideas
The words were never your own
Thoughts from someone else
Who went before
But your feelings are yours
To shine and cast a light
On the expressions you need
To communicate from
Deep within your heart and soul
Because that's where
The truth originates
Not from the ego

Let wise, soulful
Expressions inspire
But don't let them shape you
Apply your own twist
Be original
Create your own you
Express yourself

Armed with confidence
Courage in my heart
And hope by my side
I have faith in the
Strength of my being
Trustfully knowing that
The truth in my heart
Will conquer all
How fearless is this
Warrior of Love

EPILOGUE

It was lovely of you to travel with me through the landscapes of my mind. This ever expanding journey of exploring my subconscious is a fun ride.

My hope is that you can find a way to connect to the divine source that is deep within, so that you too can set sail into the sunset of your heart. I hope that you find what you are searching for.

May your spirit sparkle with excitement and send you on your way to destiny. With crystal clear focus and pure intentions, life will be on your side.